WORLD OF INSECTS
Beetles

by Colleen Sexton

BLASTOFF! 2 READERS

BELLWETHER MEDIA • MINNEAPOLIS, MN

Note to Librarians, Teachers, and Parents:

Blastoff! Readers are carefully developed by literacy experts and combine standards-based content with developmentally appropriate text.

Level 1 provides the most support through repetition of high-frequency words, light text, predictable sentence patterns, and strong visual support.

Level 2 offers early readers a bit more challenge through varied simple sentences, increased text load, and less repetition of high-frequency words.

Level 3 advances early-fluent readers toward fluency through increased text and concept load, less reliance on visuals, longer sentences, and more literary language.

Whichever book is right for your reader, Blastoff! Readers are the perfect books to build confidence and encourage a love of reading that will last a lifetime!

This edition first published in 2007 by Bellwether Media.

No part of this publication may be reproduced in whole or in part without written permission of the publisher. For information regarding permission, write to Bellwether Media Inc., Attention: Permissions Department, Post Office Box 1C, Minnetonka, MN 55345-9998.

Library of Congress Cataloging-in-Publication Data
Sexton, Colleen A.
  Beetles / by Colleen Sexton.
    p. cm. — (World of insects)
Summary: "Simple text accompanied by full-color photographs give an upclose look at beetles. Intended for kindergarten through third grade students"—Provided by publisher.
  Includes bibliographical references and index.
  ISBN-13: 978-1-60014-050-1 (hardcover : alk. paper)
  ISBN-10: 1-60014-050-5 (hardcover : alk. paper)
  1. Beetles—Juvenile literature. I. Title.

QL576.2.S49 2007
595.76—dc22   2006034960

Text copyright © 2007 by Bellwether Media.
SCHOLASTIC, CHILDREN'S PRESS, and associated logos are trademarks and/or registered trademarks of Scholastic Inc.
Printed in the United States of America.

Contents

Beetles are **insects**. Beetles
have a hard outer body.

antennas

Beetles have **antennas**.
Beetles use their antennas
to smell and feel things.

jaws

Beetles have strong jaws
for eating.

6

Some beetles can hold food or fight other insects with their jaws.

Beetles have six legs. Some beetles have long, thin legs for running.

Some beetles have strong,
short legs for digging.

Some beetles have claws
or sticky feet for climbing.

paddles

Some beetles have legs
with paddles for swimming.

Beetles have two soft wings and two hard wings.

Many beetles fly. They use their soft wings to fly.

Beetles fold their hard wings over their soft wings. Their hard wings protect their body.

Their hard wings meet in a straight line down their back.

Beetles come in many sizes.

This **giant longhorn beetle** can grow longer than your hand.

17

Beetles come in many shapes.

Beetles come in many colors.

Many beetles **blend** in with their **surroundings**.

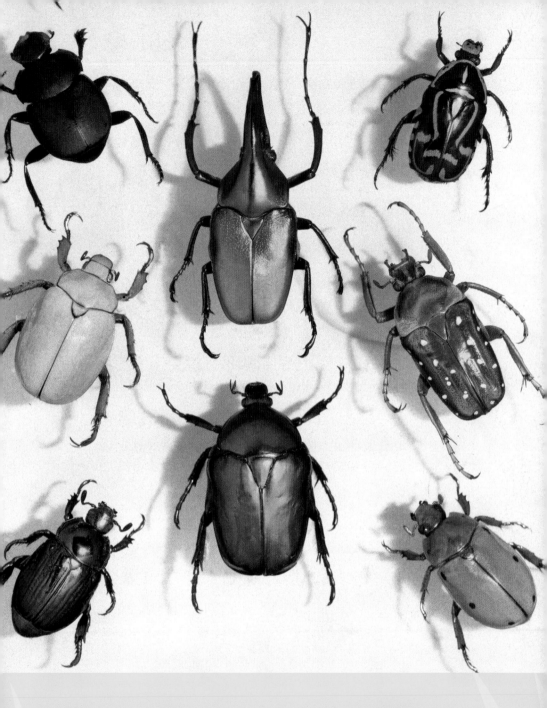

The world has more beetles
than any other kind of animal.

Glossary

antennas—the feelers on an insect's head; insects use their antennas to touch and smell things.

blend—when something looks so much like the things around it that it is hard to see

giant longhorn beetle—a kind of beetle that lives in South America; it can grow to be more than 6 inches (16 centimeters) long.

insect—a small animal with a hard outer body that is divided into three parts; most insects also have six legs, and two or four wings.

surroundings—the area around something; many beetles have colors that match their surroundings.

To Learn More

AT THE LIBRARY
Carle, Eric. *The Very Clumsy Click Beetle*. New York:
Philomel Books, 1999.

Pallotta, Jerry, and David Biedrzycki. *The Beetle
Alphabet Book*. Watertown, Mass.: Charlesbridge,
2004.

Stefoff, Rebecca. *Beetle*. New York: Benchmark
Books, 1997.

Unstead, Sue. *The Beautiful Beetle Book*. Columbus,
Ohio: Waterbird Books, 2005.

ON THE WEB
Learning more about beetles
is as easy as 1, 2, 3.

1. Go to www.factsurfer.com

2. Enter "beetles" into search box.

3. Click the "Surf" button and you will see a list of
   related web sites.

With factsurfer.com, finding more information is just
a click away.

Index

The photographs in this book are reproduced through the courtesy of: Dawn Hudson, front cover; Chris Fourie, p. 4; Tammy McAllister, p. 5; Alexander M. Omelko, p. 6; Paul R. Sterry/Alamy, p. 7; Ian McKinnell/Alamy, p. 8; Roger Eritja/Alamy, p. 9; Paul Bodea, p. 10; blickwinkel/Alamy, p. 11; Maximilian Weinzierl/Alamy, p. 12; Arco Images/Alamy, p. 13; Christian Musat, p. 14; George Grall/Getty Images, p. 15; altrendo nature/Getty Images, pp. 16, 20; Michael Schindel/Alamy, p. 17; Kevin Schafer/Alamy, p. 18; Pletnyakov Peter, p. 19; Edwin L. Wisherd/Getty Images, p. 21.